Also available in this series from Quadrille:

the little book of
MIND
-FUL-
NESS

the little book of
QUIET

the little book of
FRIENDSHIP

the little book of
LOVE

the little book of
CONFIDENCE

the little book of
MINDFUL
TRAVEL

the little book of
HAPPINESS

Edited by
Alison Davies

Hardie Grant

QUADRILLE

*"Be happy for this moment.
This moment is your life."*

OMAR KHAYYAM

What is Happiness?

Happiness is many things to many people. It can be lots of small pleasures, a general feeling of contentment or that moment when the heart soars.

"Now and then it's good to pause in our pursuit of happiness and just be happy."

GUILLAUME APOLLINAIRE

Dictionary definition of 'happiness':

a sense of well-being, joy or contentment.

How do *you* put happiness into words?

It cannot be defined. It's not a set formula for all but a unique quest where the journey is as important as the final destination. Many have fallen in their pursuit of happiness, tempted from the path by the glimmer of external treasures which provide only a fleeting and superficial glimpse of joy.

Finding happiness

To find true happiness you first need to find yourself.

Ask yourself:

- Who are you, really, truly and honestly?

- What makes your heart sing and gives your life purpose?

Therein lies the overflowing cup of joy that is your Holy Grail.

Happiness

It is a fleeting thing.
You search for it in vain and then,
while wondering where time has gone
you catch a glimpse and know
you saw it, then.

Stare from a window as the music plays
and catch the moment you become aware.
Maybe this time a sense will help you stay,
see this or that, a thought you recognize;
a feeling you can't analyse. A joy,

a fleeting thing.

VIV APPLE

Stop and let it be

When the feeling of happiness rushes through you, just stop, feel and be in that moment.

Happiness is intangible. It is a feeling, a moment that impacts your being and life. It is something you can't put in a pocket and save for later; it is something that can often feel out of reach.

"Happiness is a butterfly, which when pursued, is always just beyond your grasp, but which, if you will sit down quietly, may alight upon you."

NATHANIEL HAWTHORNE

Happiness – the facts

- The hippocampus is the area of the brain responsible for happiness.

- The neurotransmitter serotonin, which is synthesized from the amino acid tryptophan, helps to stabilize mood and regulate sleep patterns.

- The neurotransmitter dopamine also helps control emotional responses and the brain's reward and pleasure centres.

Together, serotonin and dopamine are a mood-boosting team that make us feel happy and balanced.

You can increase your levels of serotonin and dopamine by including turkey, eggs, dark chocolate and green tea in your daily diet. Other dopamine-boosting foods include almonds, avocados, bananas and chicken.

*"Keep your face to the sunshine
and you cannot see a shadow."*

HELEN KELLER

According to research, twenty minutes outside in the sunshine boosts the mood and increases levels of happiness.

*"Happiness is good health
and a bad memory."*

INGRID BERGMAN

Healthy people are twenty per cent happier than average

You can make your brain happier by exercising, as this produces proteins and endorphins which interact with opiate receptors, giving a natural 'high'.

The Danes do it best!

The World Happiness Report measures levels of happiness throughout the world, looking at variables such as generosity, life expectancy, freedom to make choices, and trust. The report is published by the United Nations Sustainable Development Solutions Network.

According to the 2017 report, Norway is the happiest country, closely followed by Denmark, Iceland and Switzerland.

" Our greatest happiness does not depend on the condition of life in which chance has placed us, but is always the result of a good conscience, good health, occupation, and freedom in all just pursuits."

THOMAS JEFFERSON

Our genes influence fifty per cent of how we feel; a further ten per cent is affected by outside circumstances such as income and environment, leaving forty per cent which is influenced by day-to-day activities and the choices we make.

"Faith is to believe what you do not see; the reward of this faith is to see what you believe."

SAINT AUGUSTINE

Happiness is universal and timeless. It's something we are all searching for, and was just as important to our ancestors as it featured in mythologies around the world. Folklore is littered with deities and spiritual beings who either represent joy, or who serve to bring this feeling to those on earth. These gods and goddesses were worshipped in different ways. Some were given offerings and rituals, while others had statues and artwork created in their honour. The Ancients saw happiness as something external to be obtained through being pro-active and appeasing the deities with magical rites and practices.

"It is folly for a man to pray to the gods for that which he has the power to obtain by himself."

EPICURUS

Happy gods

Baldur is the Norse god of light, joy and brightness, and son of Odin and Frigga. A beautiful being in appearance and nature, he was liked by all the gods except the trickster Loki, who ultimately killed him with an arrow made of mistletoe. Luckily he was resurrected and served to spread harmony through the land.

Budai, also known as the 'Laughing Buddha', has evolved over time in Chinese mythology as a god of happiness. Always smiling or laughing, he's also depicted with a large protruding belly which is a symbol of abundance and joy. He carries with him a sack which contains the sadness of the world, along with a heap of treasures, including sweets for the children, rice crops and other gifts. A protector of children and a symbol of true contentment, statues of Budai can be found in many sacred buildings and temples.

Euphrosyne was one of the three Graces in Greek mythology and a daughter of the god Zeus. The goddess of joy and mirth, she and her sisters were created to bring pleasure to the earth. Usually pictured dancing in a circle with her sisters, Euphrosyne was called upon to raise the spirits and encourage the flow of happiness.

Hathor is the Egyptian goddess of joy, love and motherhood. Adored by the people, Hathor was also known as 'Mistress of the West' and was thought to welcome the dead into the afterlife. Linked to fertility and protection, Hathor had many roles and was closely associated with pleasurable pursuits such as dance and music. A true embodiment of happiness, she was also known as the 'Mistress of Life', for she encapsulated many aspects of the world, and all the good things in it.

"Happy is he who hath in himself praise and wisdom in life."

HÁVAMÁL

"Most folks are as happy as they make up their minds to be."

ABRAHAM LINCOLN

Happiness comes from within

Happiness is not just a feeling, it is also an attitude, it is a choice. True happiness cannot be captured through the affirmation or actions of others. Although we can be inspired by the people around us, we have to find and feel happiness for ourselves.

Choose to be happy.

How do you find happiness?

- Is it something external that you seek, like the Holy Grail?

- Or does it lurk inside somewhere; a gem of light hidden away until you find the right words to free it from its prison?

- Is it something that you create?

- A masterpiece made up of thoughts, words and deeds?

- What are the rules, the workings of this joy machine?

The mechanics of happiness may at first seem complicated but look again: you'll see that to be happy is to be comfortable in your own skin. To enjoy the simple things in life and engage with the world around you. Most importantly, be kind to yourself and others.

Practise smiling

Even if you don't feel like it.

Force yourself to smile in front of a mirror at least twice a day.

It may feel strange at first, but persevere.

Exaggerate the upward curve of your lips and stretch your mouth into a wide grin.

As your face changes, so your heart changes until the smile reaches your eyes and you feel warm inside.

Eventually you'll notice a difference in your thoughts and emotions. Like medicine for the soul, the smile will work its magic until you find your happy place.

Smile!

"A smile is happiness you'll find right under your nose."

TOM WILSON

"The happiness of life is made up of minute fractions – the little, soon-forgotten charities of a kiss or a smile, a kind look or heartfelt compliment."

SAMUEL TAYLOR COLERIDGE

A smile is contagious –
pass it on freely and often

Play a game and count the number of smiles you get in return for your own throughout the day. That in itself will give you even more to smile about!

"The talent for being happy is appreciating and liking what you have, instead of what you don't have."

ANONYMOUS

Always look on the bright side...

Positive thinking is like domino rolling: once you set off on a positive train of thought it will gather momentum and speed, until you reach your destination – happiness.

Try not to dwell on the past or get stuck in a cycle of 'what if'

There is always a reason for the choices we make so embrace your decisions and know that they were right for you.

While it's not always easy to look on the bright side, it is beneficial to health and general well-being. Researchers have found that optimists tend to live longer and have lower rates of depression and stress. Cardiovascular health is improved and there is less risk of heart disease, and greater resistance to everyday ailments such as the common cold. It's thought the reason for this is a positive outlook; so when an optimist encounters a stressful situation, their upbeat attitude means they handle it better than someone with a negative countenance.

"Once you replace negative thoughts with positive ones, you'll start having positive results."

WILLIE NELSON

Kintsugi

This is the ancient Japanese art of recognizing the beauty of broken things.

For the last 500 years the Japanese have restored their broken plates and cups through kintsugi, otherwise known as 'golden joinery'. Craftsmen replace broken pieces of china with a lacquer mixed with gold, silver or platinum.

There is much to be learnt from kintsugi. The most important lesson being that we can learn from our negative experiences, take the best from them and know that these experiences make each person unique and precious.

Life doesn't have to be perfect
to be wonderful.

"Sandwich every bit of criticism between two layers of praise."

MARY KAY ASH

As humans we have a habit of berating ourselves, of beating ourselves up at almost every opportunity. We do this through our internal critic, the inner voice always ready with an acerbic comment. We wouldn't talk to our friends like this. We wouldn't talk to strangers like this. Stop the internal critic from chipping away at your happiness NOW!

Silence the inner critic

- The minute your mind presents you with a negative comment, shout 'STOP!' in your head.

- Count to five slowly and breathe.

- Negate the effect of the comment by saying something positive to override it, for example 'I am wonderful just the way I am' or 'I am happy with myself'.

- Repeat the positive affirmation several times; this serves to banish the criticism for good.

- Take a deep breath, smile and enjoy your victory.

" The art of being happy lies in the power of extracting happiness from common things."

HENRY WARD BEECHER

Remember that you can start right now

Don't expect happiness to always find you, or even hang around waiting for everything to fall into place.

Happiness is a choice.

Stop looking for it and start living it.

"Happiness cannot be travelled to, owned, earned, worn or consumed. Happiness is the spiritual experience of living every minute with love, grace and gratitude."

DENIS WAITLEY

Happiness is letting go of what you think life is supposed to look like, and just celebrating everything that it is.

"Think of all the beauty still left around you and be happy."

ANNE FRANK - TUESDAY, 7 MARCH 1944

Engage the senses

See the magic in the world around you.

Breathe it in.

Touch it.

Taste it.

Smell it.

Live it.

Connect with the environment

Write a short paragraph about your journey into work/doing the school run/taking the dog for a walk.

Now imagine you're retracing your steps. Go through the journey in your mind and engage all of your senses. Take note of what you saw, what you could hear, smell, touch, taste and how you felt.

Rewrite your journey, this time engaging the senses fully.

Read both accounts. The first may include some level of description, but the second will have more colour and depth, making it vibrant.

Imagine the difference if you engage your senses every day. Mundane tasks and activities become instantly more attractive and exciting, which promotes a feeling of contentment and wonder.

Some days you just have to create your own sunshine.

"I'm not one of those complicated mixed-up cats. I'm not looking for the secret to life... I just go on from day to day, taking what comes."

FRANK SINATRA

Don't sweat the small stuff –
it's ALL small stuff.

To be comfortable in your own skin you need to be able to breathe, to let loose, to relax and be flexible. This becomes impossible if everything is set in stone, if you're rigid in thought and mind.

- Practise stretching; it's good for the body and soul.

- Daydream often; it's the key to a positive frame of mind.

- Catnap when you can.

- Laugh with all your heart.

- Learn to laugh at yourself.

> *"The habit of being happy enables one to be freed, or largely freed, from the domination of outward conditions."*

ROBERT LOUIS STEVENSON

Thoughts are powerful.
They shape the present
and the future. If you can
think 'happy' you'll be happy.

The mind finds it hard to distinguish between fact and fiction, which makes it easy to reprogram the way you think and feel using cleverly worded affirmations.

Affirmations

- Pick an affirmation that feels right for you and repeat it for three minutes every morning and evening. This works best if you're in front of a mirror, so try it when you're getting ready in the morning (putting on make-up/shaving/washing) and when you're preparing for bed.

- Say the affirmation out loud, emphasizing the words.

- Say it as if you mean it.

- Write it down and pin it somewhere you'll see it every day.

15 'happy' affirmations

I am happy with who I am

I am happy being me

I love my life and it loves me

I am filled with positive energy

I am joyful

Every day my world is a happier place

I radiate joy

I am thankful for the gift that is my life

I shine with happiness

I choose happiness

I enjoy every moment of my life

I deserve to be happy

Every day is a joyful experience

Happiness is second nature to me

I am filled with light and love

"*Mindfulness helps you go home to the present. And every time you go there and recognize a condition of happiness that you have, happiness comes.*"

THICH NHAT HANH

Live in the moment

Every second is a precious
opportunity for joy.

Stop watching the clock

Sometimes we can be taken by surprise at how quickly time passes and can feel panicked with how little time we have left for ourselves.

So don't live by your clock – there are moments when all we need is to sit and contemplate, or simply have an extra-long lie-in.

Don't feel guilty, stop counting the seconds and live for the moment.

"Time you enjoy wasting is not wasted time."

MARTHE TROLY-CURTIN

"Sometimes your joy is the source of your smile, but sometimes your smile can be the source of your joy."

THICH NHAT HANH

Surround yourself with positive people

Keeping the company of optimists increases your personal happiness. This is because positive emotions have a tendency to rub off on our own mood, meaning it's hard to remain sad when those around you are full of joy. Studies have shown that every 'happy' friend increases your probability of happiness by nine per cent.

"Some cause happiness wherever they go; others whenever they go."

OSCAR WILDE

Spread the joy

Tell a joke, do something silly, or
simply smile to share your feeling
of happiness.

"*Beauty is an ecstasy; it is as simple as hunger. There is really nothing to be said about it. It is like the perfume of a rose: you can smell it and that is all.*"

W. SOMERSET MAUGHAM

"Happiness is the secret to all beauty.
There is no beauty without happiness."

CHRISTIAN DIOR

The scent of joy

Our sense of smell is one of the most powerful. It evokes memories of long-lost places and times. Like magic it has the power to summon the faces of those who were once dear to us and the ability to transport us back to a special moment: the first stirrings of attraction that blossomed into romance, or the joy of a hazy summer's day. Scientists have discovered the reason for this. There's a direct link within the brain between memory and smell and this link works much faster than our other senses. The olfactory bulb which processes smell communicates with those parts of the brain that store emotional memories. Over time and with conditioning we learn to associate certain scents with a feeling.

This is a natural reaction and we often cannot define the distinct memory that causes the emotional response, whether positive or negative.

There are, however, some fragrances that have a universal effect on how we feel. For example, in studies it's been shown that lemon or peppermint tends to make people feel more alert, while menthol scents in general clear the head and give those subjected to them instant clarity and vision. The smell of coffee brewing fires the mind and motivates us into action, while vanilla and chocolate provide an air of seduction and are thought to increase allure. While we're all different, and there is no set combination of smells that guarantees happiness, there are some specific scents that can help to lift the mood.

Joyful whiffs

Orange

Lemon

Bergamot

Geranium

Jasmine

Pine

Lavender

Vanilla

Rose

Rosemary

Scentsational tips

Create your own smell library. Make a list of scents that remind you of happy times, whether these are from childhood or more recent memories. Wherever possible, try and recreate those aromas. For example, if the smell of bread baking reminds you of the fun times you had in the kitchen with your mum, make a point of baking bread at least once a week.

- Experiment with fragrance. Invest in essential oils and add them to baths or massage oils. Make a note of how they make you feel. Once you've identified your key 'happy' oils, add them to other things such as ironing water or floor wash, or burn them in a little water to create a 'joyful' atmosphere in every room.

- Go for a walk in nature and breathe in the scents of your surroundings. Even smelling the flowers in your garden or local park will boost the mood.

" *Music is a moral law. It gives soul to the universe, wings to the mind, flight to the imagination, and charm and gaiety to life and to everything.* "

PLATO

According to research, the music you listen to has an effect on your mood. Two weeks of enjoying upbeat, joyful tracks has a positive effect on the way you feel and can turn a frown upside down. Even sad music has its place, acting as a comfort and providing empathy through times of stress.

Theme tune

Pick a happy theme tune and make it your own. Start by making a list of all the songs that make you feel good. Go for upbeat tunes that are guaranteed to get you on the dance floor. Choose the one that makes you feel the happiest and play it to remind you of those positive feelings. Enjoy the freedom of movement, and have a boogie as you do this.

Whenever you feel sad or in need of a happiness injection, replay the song in your head. Imagine turning up the stereo in your mind and relive the joyful experience of grooving to your 'happy' theme tune.

Dance like there's no-one watching!

"If you can't get rid of the skeleton in your closet, you'd best teach it to dance."

GEORGE BERNARD SHAW

"Sunshine is delicious, rain is refreshing, wind braces us up, snow is exhilarating; there is really no such thing as bad weather, only different kinds of good weather."

JOHN RUSKIN

The joy of nature

Reconnecting with nature is good for mind, body and soul. It elevates mood, helps to combat depression and improves self-esteem. Studies have shown that children with Attention Deficit Hyperactivity Disorder (ADHD) have benefited greatly from wildlife interaction, and the effects are far-reaching. In general, nature lovers are happier and healthier than those who have limited contact with the natural world.

"The tree which moves some to tears of joy is in the eyes of others only a green thing that stands in the way. Some see nature all ridicule and deformity ... and some scarce see nature at all. But to the eyes of the man of imagination, nature is imagination itself."

WILLIAM BLAKE

Stand with your back against the trunk of a tree. Feel the roughness of the bark against the palms of your hands. Look up into the boughs and marvel at the beauty of the leaves. Breathe and notice the deep swell of joy that rises from your belly.

"The beautiful spring came; and when Nature resumes her loveliness, the human soul is apt to revive also."

HARRIET ANN JACOBS

Engaging with the environment, and appreciating the natural beauty of your surroundings, brings fresh perspective. When combined with some kind of 'wildlife' interaction such as sowing flower seeds or feeding the birds, the benefits become reinforced because you're doing something physical and giving back to the earth and its creatures.

'Friluftsliv' (pron. 'fri-loofts-live') is a Nordic philosophy celebrating the outdoors and appreciating nature.

First coined in 1859, 'friluftsliv' is now ingrained in Nordic culture. It directly translates to 'free-air life' and embodies the idea that returning to nature is returning home.

On the Heights

I den øde sæterstue
al min rige fangst jeg sanker;
der er krak og der er grue,
friluftsliv for mine tanker.

In the lonely mountain farm,
My abundant catch I take.
There is a hearth, and table,
And friluftsliv for my thoughts.

HENRIK IBSEN

Throughout human existence, there are things we do to guarantee our happiness. Forming relationships, looking after friends and family and maintaining health and well-being are a part of this. There are other things too, simple customs and rituals that we perform, sometimes without thought, to ensure that we remain content. These things can be old family traditions passed down through the generations, or new rituals that we've developed over time.

"Joy in looking and comprehending is nature's most beautiful gift."

ALBERT EINSTEIN

Customs and rituals

Wishing trees were a popular way for ancient civilizations to secure happiness. Usually a fir or pine tree would be planted near the home and watered often with wine. The planter would take the time to talk to the tree and ask for joyful blessings on their nearest and dearest. Often wishes would be made for things that would bring happiness, and the leaves of the tree would be rubbed between finger and thumb to release the scent and send the wish to the heavens.

During the Middle Ages silver objects were used as talismans for happiness. They had to be 100 per cent silver, and were left out in the light of the full moon to be cleansed. They would then be wrapped carefully in a piece of muslin or other material, and carried about the person as a charm for good fortune and joy.

Wassailing was an ancient Twelfth Night ritual: a bowl of spicy brew was passed from person to person while various wishes for good health and happiness were pronounced. Traditionally the wassail cup was raised to the spirits of the fruit tree and participants made merry while celebrating the changing seasons and the coming of spring. An Anglo-Saxon custom, it is still used today as a way of securing happiness for the year ahead.

In Hungary, one New Year's tradition thought to ensure a happy, healthy year ahead involves washing your face in a bowl of cold water with a red apple floating in it.

"When you rise in the morning, give thanks for the light, for your life, for your strength. Give thanks for your food and for the joy of living. If you see no reason to give thanks, the fault lies in yourself."

TECUMSEH

Being grateful is like taking 'happy' medicine every day. It helps us value the things we do have, rather than focusing on those which appear out of reach. It puts life into perspective and reminds us we are fabulous and unique. This has an uplifting effect on our mood and how we engage with the world around us.

"A grateful heart is a beginning of greatness. It is an expression of humility. It is a foundation for the development of such virtues as prayer, faith, courage, contentment, happiness, love, and well-being."

JAMES E. FAUST

Get rolling!

Be grateful today for one thing, then tomorrow challenge yourself to be grateful for two, then three, then four. Like a tiny snowball as it rolls down the hill, as the days progress your grateful attitude will pick up pace and you'll collect other positive emotions along the way, until finally you'll be so swollen with happiness you'll explode and shower everyone around you with joyful light!

The science behind practising gratitude

Stress hormones such as cortisol are twenty-three per cent lower in people who show gratitude. The same people are likely to produce more oxytocin, the hormone associated with love and feeling good.

"I would maintain that thanks are the highest form of thought, and that gratitude is happiness doubled by wonder."

G.K. CHESTERTON

Count your blessings

Create a gratitude box in which you can store all your blessings. Either invest in a gift box, or take an old shoe box and decorate it with pictures and ribbons to make it look special. Every day make a note of something you're thankful for and add it to the box. If you can think of more than one thing, even better! By doing this, you'll get into the habit of reviewing your life and all the good things you've got going on. This kind of practice is the key to a happy outlook and attracting even more sunshine into your world. Remember, whenever you need a boost, rifle through the box and remind yourself how lucky you are.

"Let us be grateful to people who make us happy; they are the charming gardeners who make our souls blossom."

MARCEL PROUST

Happiness finds you through gratitude

Open your heart to gratitude and it will change every aspect of your life. You'll become more likeable and loving, which affects your relationships, helping you to bond with new people and cement existing ties. Your working relationships will progress like a dream and because you're feeling more relaxed you'll be able to charm the birds from the trees (should the need arise).

Positive energy will radiate from every part of your being, making you more optimistic and fun to be around. This in turn means you'll have more fun, and where fun resides happiness follows.

"Happiness is a choice that requires effort at times."

AESCHYLUS

"I am what happened to me;
I am what I choose to become."

CARL JUNG

Give thanks for the bad stuff too. Life may hand you lemons, but even if you can't make lemonade you can still appreciate the fruits provided. Just say 'THANK YOU' to the universe as loudly as possible. Vent your anger in gratitude because every situation, every moment, joyous or heart-breaking, teaches you something.

The five gifts

The ancient Egyptians believed in the concept of gratitude. Even the poor were encouraged to give thanks for their blessings using a ritual known as 'the five gifts of Hathor'. The left hand was used by labourers to harvest the crops daily, so it was considered sacred. Each finger on this hand represented a blessing in their life, which would be marked and counted regularly as a reminder to be thankful and as a way of honouring the goddess Hathor.

*" There is only one happiness
in this life, to love and be loved."*

GEORGE SAND

When we fall in love, twelve areas of the brain light up and release a combination of powerful chemicals which produce a euphoric feeling. These 'happy' chemicals affect the brain's cognitive centres almost instantly.

Say 'I love you' often.

It will not wear out and it's guaranteed to put a smile on your face and theirs.

Remember, too, to say it to yourself.

Love yourself and others will take your lead.

"*Remember that the happiest people are not those getting more, but those giving more.*"

H. JACKSON BROWN, JR.

What happens when we hug?

The hormone oxytocin is released into the bloodstream. This happy hormone does a number of things, from reducing stress and anxiety to lowering blood pressure and improving memory. Hugging is also essential for developing empathy, and research has proved that over time this can make you a more compassionate person.

Interesting hug fact:

It's unusual to give a hug
and not get one in return.

Being married can increase your levels of happiness. According to research replicated around the world, married couples and those in civil partnerships rate their life satisfaction and general contentment higher than those who are single.

" *The secret to a happy marriage is
if you can be at peace with someone
within four walls, if you are content
because the one you love is near to you,
either upstairs or downstairs, or in the
same room, and you feel that warmth
that you don't find very often, then that
is what love is all about.* "

SIR BRUCE FORSYTH

"Happiness is having a large, loving, caring, close-knit family in another city."

GEORGE BURNS

"Friendship is the source of the greatest pleasures, and without friends even the most agreeable pursuits become tedious."

THOMAS AQUINAS

The need to belong is fundamental to our happiness. Those who are highly social tend to be happier than those who mix less. There is also evidence that people with lots of friends tend to be more optimistic and have lower stress levels, because they turn to their friends for support.

" We secure our friends not by accepting favours but by doing them."

THUCYDIDES

Joy vouchers

You can't buy these from a shop.
They're priceless.

Write a list of things that you can do for friends and family to make them smile. Choose simple things that are free but require time and effort. For example, doing the shopping, washing the car or cooking a nice meal.

Write out a set of vouchers for each person, bundle them together and tie with ribbon for the perfect present with a personal twist.

The good news is that this gift works two ways: they'll be happy to receive your love and you'll be happy sharing it!

"*To be kind to all, to like many and love a few, to be needed and wanted by those we love, is certainly the nearest we can come to happiness.*"

INUIT PROVERB

Happiness is contagious

If our friends are happy, it's likely to affect how we feel as we share in their pleasure.

"Friendship improves happiness and abates misery, by the doubling of our joy and the dividing of our grief."

MARCUS TULLIUS CICERO

The philosopher Aristotle distinguished different types of friendship. He described friendships for mutual utility and friendships for mutual goodwill, and claimed that the hallmark of true friendship is reciprocal altruism – a form of sharing kindness that results in mutual benefit.

"*Animals are such agreeable friends – they ask no questions; they pass no criticisms.*"

GEORGE ELIOT

Having pets makes you a happier person. Spending time with animals is therapeutic, lowers stress levels and also combats loneliness, along with the added joy it brings in loving and being loved unconditionally.

"Until one has loved an animal, a part of one's soul remains unawakened."

ANATOLE FRANCE

" There are two means of refuge from the miseries of life: music and cats."

ALBERT SCHWEITZER

Engage your imagination and express yourself in new ways to trigger happy vibes.

"It is in the compelling zest of high adventure and of victory, and in creative action, that man finds his supreme joys."

ANTOINE DE SAINT-EXUPÉRY

Being creative means we live in the moment, we become immersed and engaged in an activity which also helps us express how we feel and tap into our emotions. When you're in the creative flow, you're in the flow of life and you learn to appreciate every second.

"*The creation of something new is not accomplished by the intellect but by the play instinct acting from inner necessity. The creative mind plays with the objects it loves.*"

CARL JUNG

Play often

Do things you enjoy and encourage a childlike sense of fun in everyday activities.

"It is requisite for the relaxation of the mind that we make use, from time to time, of playful deeds and jokes."

THOMAS AQUINAS

Experience exhilaration

Dare to daydream.

"I'm not much of a math and science guy. I spent most of my time in school daydreaming and managed to turn it into a living."

GEORGE LUCAS

When we drift into daydream we access our imagination and begin to create a different world. We generate pleasurable emotions and we create aspirations. Most importantly, we visualize the future in exciting new ways, which allows us to think that anything is possible, and this belief then becomes our reality.

"Visualization is daydreaming with a purpose."

BO BENNETT

"Visualize this thing that you want, see it, feel it, believe in it. Make your mental blue print, and begin to build."

ROBERT COLLIER

If you can picture what you want to happen and how you'd like to be, then you'll make it a reality. The more you engage your imagination and invest in that picture, the more creative energy you generate.

This is the key to visualization.

See yourself happy and imagine how that feels.

Conjure up joyful emotions. Experience them. Feel them permeate through your body. Do this daily until it becomes second nature.

Be happy being you
and express yourself.

Put pen to paper.

Give yourself an allotted time every day and write how you feel. Treat this as a journal and let all your thoughts and emotions flow. Getting into the habit of expressing how you truly feel helps you get in touch with your creative side.

"Life begins at the end of your comfort zone."

NEALE DONALD WALSCH

Step outside your comfort zone.

"Be willing to step outside your comfort zone once in a while; take the risks in life that seem worth taking. The ride might not be as predictable as if you'd just planted your feet and stayed put, but it will be a heck of a lot more interesting."

EDWARD WHITACRE, JR.

Do something different, even something small.

Take a new route to work, grab your morning coffee from a different vendor or try reading a new magazine or broadsheet. Striking out in this way encourages you to take a creative approach in all areas of your life.

"Happiness lies in the joy of achievement and the thrill of creative effort."

FRANKLIN D. ROOSEVELT

Do what you love.

" Success is not the key to happiness.
Happiness is the key to success.
If you love what you are doing,
you will be successful."

ALBERT SCHWEITZER

Find something that brings you joy and turn it into a career, and you'll never work a day in your life.

"*Never permit a dichotomy to rule your life, a dichotomy in which you hate what you do so you can have pleasure in your spare time. Look for a situation in which your work will give you as much happiness as your spare time.*"

PABLO PICASSO

"Being happy is of the utmost importance. Success in anything is through happiness."

MAHARISHI MAHESH YOGI

While we may not be successful in all our endeavours, if we choose to do something we enjoy and put our heart and soul into it, then we will be happy and that is a success in itself.

Question: Which is best, the happy man or the successful man?

Answer: They are the same, for the happy man is successful in his happiness and the successful man is happy in his success.

They are inexorably linked; two friends walking hand in hand along life's footpath.

Embrace your victories, big and small

Learning to be happy with what you have and who you are – that is true success.

"*Success is getting and achieving what you want. Happiness is wanting and being content with what you get.*"

BERNARD MELTZER

"Cheerfulness keeps up a kind of daylight in the mind, filling it with a steady and perpetual serenity."

JOSEPH ADDISON

There is no standard recipe for happiness, nor is there an equation, simple or otherwise. The secret to being in this state of joy is far more complex and made up of a balance of ingredients which differs for each individual. There is, however, a formula that guarantees contentment and it is this: learn what makes you happy, then find it every day. Hold on to it, but don't cling to it or you will suffocate the emotion.

Happiness needs room to breathe and grow. Like a tree, it stands the test of time but it also changes, shifting and turning with each season. What made you happy when you were five might not make you happy when you're fifty. Then again, you might return to childish pursuits to rekindle those blissful emotions.

The choice is yours, and that is the key

Happiness *is* a choice, conscious or otherwise. It's that feeling of the cup overflowing. A cheerful approach to life. A general satisfaction with your lot, whatever it may be or however it presents itself.

"Happiness is a place between too little and too much."

FINNISH PROVERB

"If you want happiness for an hour – take a nap.

If you want happiness for a day – go fishing.

If you want happiness for a year – inherit a fortune.

If you want happiness for a lifetime – help someone else."

CHINESE PROVERB

Carpe diem: 'Seize the day'

Translated from Latin, this philosophy is commonly used to encompass the enjoyment of the pleasure of a moment without concern for the future or the past.

"There is no glory in star or blossom till looked upon by a loving eye; There is no fragrance in April breezes till breathed with joy as they wander by."

WILLIAM C. BRYANT

Be flexible, open and generous with your happiness and you'll be delighted daily.

PAGE REFERENCES

Page 56: Frank, Anne. ©ANNE FRANK FONDS Basel, Switzerland

Page 80: Maugham, W. Somerset., *Cakes and Ale* (Doubleday, Doran & Company, Inc, 1958)

Page 98: Jacobs, Harriet Ann., *Incidents in the Life of a Slave Girl* (Boston, 1861)

Page 115: Chesterton, G.K., *The Collected Works of G.K* (Ignatius Press, 1986)

BIBLIOGRAPHY & FURTHER READING

Books

Chesterton, G.K., *The Collected Works of G.K* (Ignatius Press, 1986)

Dolan, Paul., *Happiness by Design: Finding Pleasure and Purpose in Everyday Life* (Penguin, 2015)

Frank, Anne., *The Diary of a Young Girl* (Viking, 1997)

Jacobs, Harriet Ann., *Incidents in the Life of a Slave Girl* (Boston, 1861)

Marston, Ralph., *The Daily Motivator*, greatday.com

Maugham, W. Somerset., *Cakes and Ale* (Doubleday, Doran & Company, Inc, 1958)

O'Connor, Annmarie., *The Happy Closet* (Gill & Macmillan, 2015)

Perle, Susie., *Instruction for Happiness and Success* (Quadrille, 2012)

Rowan, Tiddy., *The Little Book of Mindfulness* (Quadrille, 2013)

Rubin, Gretchen., *Happiness Project* (Harper Collins, 2011)

Sturge, Lisa., *Laugh* (Quadrille, 2017)

Tolle, Eckhart., *The Power of Now: A Guide to Spiritual Enlightenment* (Yellow Kite, 2011)

Wiking, Meik., *The Little Book of Hygge: The Danish Way to Live Well* (Penguin Life, 2016)

Documentary

Happy, Roko Belic, United States: Wadi Rum Productions, 2011.

Websites

www.projecthappiness.com

www.stylist.co.uk/travel/hygge-friluftsliv-meaning-scandinavian-danish-denmark-norwegian-health-happiness

www.worldhappiness.report

Apps

Gratitude Journal

Calm

Headspace

QUOTES ARE TAKEN FROM:

Abraham Lincoln was the sixteenth President of the United States and was assassinated in 1865.

Aeschylus was an ancient Greek playwright known as the father of tragedy.

Albert Einstein was a German-born theoretical physicist who developed the theory of relativity.

Albert Schweitzer was a French-German physician, philosopher and musician who was awarded the Nobel Peace Prize in 1952.

Anatole France was an ironic and sceptical French novelist, poet and journalist.

Anne Frank was a German-born Jewish schoolgirl, famed for her diary, published posthumously as *The Diary of a Young Girl*, describing her life while in hiding from the Nazis.

Antoine de Saint-Exupéry was a French writer and poet known for his pioneering work in aviation during the 1900s.

Bernard Meltzer was an American radio host from the 60s to the 90s.

Bo Bennett is an American doctor of social psychology, author and television presenter.

Brené Brown is an American author, scholar and orator.

Carl Jung was a Swiss psychiatrist who founded analytical psychology and whose work as been hugely influential in many fields other than his own.

Christian Dior was a French fashion designer whose legacy and designer label continue to flourish to this very day.

Denis Waitley was an American motivational speaker, writer and best-selling author of the audio series *The Psychology of Winning*.

Edward Whitacre, Jr. is the former chairman and CEO of General Motors and also served as the President of the Boy Scouts of America from 1998 to 2000.

Epicurus was an ancient Greek philosopher born in 341 BC who founded the school of philosophy called Epicureanism.

Francis Bacon was an English scientist, author and philosopher and served as Lord Chancellor of England. His work was extremely influential during the scientific revolution.

Frank Sinatra was an American, actor and singer. He was one of the most popular entertainers of the 20th century and left behind a massive catalog of iconic songs including 'My Way' and 'Come Fly with Me'.

Franklin D. Roosevelt was the thirty-second President of the United States of America.

George Bernard Shaw was an Irish playwright, critic and political activist who had a huge influence on Western theatre and culture. His works include *Pygmalion* and *Saint Joan*.

George Burns was an American comedian, actor, singer and writer.

George Eliot, pseudonym of Mary Anne Evans, was a leading English poet, novelist and journalist during the Victorian era.

George Lucas is an American film-maker best known for his creation of the Star Wars and Indiana Jones franchises.

George Sand, pseudonym of Amantine Lucie Aurore Dupin, was a French novelist during the 1800s.

G. K. Chesterton was an English writer, poet, journalist and philosopher.

Guillaume Apollinaire was a French poet, playwright and novelist at the forefront of the art scene in the early 20th century, credited with coining the term 'cubism'.

H. Jackson Brown, Jr. is an American author whose book, *Life's Little Instruction Book*, was a *New York Times* bestseller.

Harriet Ann Jacobs was an African-American writer who escaped from slavery. She was later formally freed and became an abolitionist speaker and reformer.

Hávamál is a poem in the *Codex Regius*, a collection of Old Norse poems from the Viking age, whose words are said to be those of Odin and present advice for living, proper conduct and wisdom.

Helen Keller was an American author, lecturer and political activist and was the first deaf-blind person to earn a degree.

Henrik Ibsen was a Norwegian playwright during the 19th century and is considered to be one of the founders of Modernism in theatre.

Henry Ward Beecher was an American Congregationalist clergyman and social reformer who supported the abolition of slavery.

Ingrid Bergman was a multiple award-winning Swedish actress famous for her roles in *Casablanca* and Hitchcock's *Notorious*.

James E. Faust was an American politician and religious leader.

John Ruskin was an influential British art critic, watercolourist and philanthropist during the Victorian era.

Joseph Addison was an English poet, playwright and politician during the seventeenth century.

Maharishi Mahesh Yogi developed the Transcendental Meditation technique.

Marcel Proust was a French novelist known best for his huge work *À la recherche du temps perdu* which was published in seven parts over fourteen years.

Marcus Tullius Cicero was an ancient Roman politician and lawyer and was considered one of Rome's greatest orators and prose stylists.

Marthe Troly-Curtin was the author of the Phrynette novels.

Mary Kay Ash was an American businesswoman in the 1960s and paved the way for female entrepreneurs.

Nathaniel Hawthorne was an American novelist famous for writing *The Scarlet Letter*.

Neale Donald Walsh is an American actor, screenwriter, orator and author of the series *Conversations with God*.

Nelson Mandela was the first black president of South African. He was a civil rights activist and helped bring an end to the apartheid. In 1993 he was awarded the Nobel Prize for Peace.

Omar Khayyam was a Persian scholar, astronomer and philosopher and was considered to be one of the most significant thinkers of the Middle Ages.

Oscar Wilde was an Irish novelist, playwright and poet whose works became incredibly popular in London in the 1890s.

Pablo Picasso was a Spanish painter and sculptor who is considered to be one of the most influential artists of the twentieth century.

Plato was a classical Greek philosopher, student of Socrates and teacher of Aristotle.

Ralph Marston is an American writer who runs The Daily Motivator, a website aimed at giving people a happier, more positive outlook on life.

Robert Collier was an American author of self-help books during the twentieth century.

Robert Louis Stevenson was a Scottish novelist famous for works such as *Treasure Island* and *Strange Case of Dr Jekyll and Mr Hyde*.

Saint Augustine, born 354 AD, was Christian theologian and philosopher whose work greatly influenced the growth and change of Western Christianity.

Samuel Taylor Coleridge was an English poet and founder of the Romantic Movement. He was a member of the Lake Poets, along with his friend William Wordsworth and is famed for works such as *The Rime of the Ancient Mariner*.

Sir Bruce Forsyth CBE is an English television presenter and entertainer.

St. Thomas Aquinas was an influential Italian Catholic Priest and Doctor of the Church during the 13th Century.

Tecumseh was the leader of the Shawnee Native Americans during the turn of the 19th century.

Thich Nhat Hanh is a Buddhist monk, spiritual leader, poet and peace activist.

Thomas Jefferson was the primary author of the Declaration of Independence and the third President of the United States.

Thucydides was an ancient Greek historian and general who recorded the battles between Athens and Sparta.

Tom Wilson is an American actor, artist, comedian and writer who has had a huge influence on popular culture.

Viv Apple is a poet and author from Nottingham, UK.

William Blake was a 19th century writer and artist who was an influential figure during the Romantic Age.

William Bryant was an American romantic poet, journalist and editor for 50 years of the New York *Evening Post*.

Willie Nelson is an American muscian and singer-songwriter.

W. Somerset Maugham was an English novelist, playwright and short story writer.

Publishing Director Sarah Lavelle
Editor Harriet Butt
Editorial Assistant Harriet Webster
Creative Director Helen Lewis
Series Designer Emily Lapworth
Designer Shani Travers
Production Director Vincent Smith
Production Controller Nikolaus Ginelli

First published in 2017 by Quadrille,
an imprint of Hardie Grant Publishing

Quadrille
52–54 Southwark Street
London SE1 1 UN
quadrille.com

Reprinted in 2017 (twice), 2018 (twice),
2019 (twice), 2021 (twice)
12 11 10 9

British Library Cataloguing-
in-Publication Data
A catalogue record for this book is
available from the British Library.

ISBN: 978 1 78713 112 5

Printed in China